Love

- by any definition -

A collection
of Love poems

Jean-Jacques Fournier

ISBN 978-1-79473-019-9

Publisher: FON INT.
Contact: fon.int@sympatico.ca

First edition

Photos and art references: page 164
All rights reserved
Book, cover, photos and layout designs by Marianne Dessis
© Marianne Dessis -

For all the women, I've known and loved,

and those I never got to know,

but most of all, for one of lasting love,

Marianne, till my last breath,

be my truelove!

Also by Jean-Jacques Fournier

Poetry

Issues - of black and white -
Matters - of body and soul -
Images - in shades and shadows -

Places - of loss and found -
Obliquities - of a lucid mind -
Reflexions - of a probing eye -

Issues - of black and white - *(second edition)*
Matters - of body and soul - *(second edition)*
Images - in shades and shadows - *(second edition)*

Kaleidoscope - musings of life chronicles -
A Hyphenated World - a fitting guise -
A Scent of Reality - be inherent perception -

Held Instant - on life's clock -
Conjugated People - by shade -
Chaos – a human side of man -

Contents:

54.	Body Heat - in ambrosial state -
55.	-
56.	Days Like This - reminds me now -
57.	Don't Stop - for egoist thought -
58.	Echoes - of love's yearning -
59.	Emotions - fate finds abide -
60.	Emotions - without constraint -
61.	Façade - of a love blind -
62.	Feelings - of a love's neglect -
63.	First Love - that special place -
64.	Forget Me Not - while I am here -
65.	-
66.	Friend - a singular entitlement -
67.	-
68.	Heart Disowned - in a stubborn soul -
69.	Her Love - and mine -
70.	How Will We Know - we'll not end broken hearted -
71.	-
72.	I Confess - live in a state -
73.	I love it all - irrefutably so -
74.	-
75.	I Love Rain - when it drizzles -
76.	-
77.	I Wish You Love - more than you'd miss -
78.	If Only - I'd known how -
79.	Impressions - of a lover's intentions -
80.	In Whom We Trust - a pledge unyielding -
81.	-
82.	Just Knowing - who you are -
83.	-
84.	L'Amour Que J'Aime Et Que J'Adore - the one I love, and so adore -
85.	-
86.	Lady In Silk - can't disguise -
87.	-
88.	Libertines - in a heedless ambivalence -
89.	-
90.	Limbo - a place of mind -
91.	-
92.	Lost Feelings - at play -
93.	Love - of my life -
94.	Love For Sale - on any scale -
95.	Love For Share - once for sale -

96. Love The More - as ne'er before -
97. Love To Share - any which way -
98. -
99. Love To Share - as the heart bids -
100. Lovebirds - be an example -
101. -
102. Lover - to make -
103. -
104. Lovers - ever so -
105. Loving You - before and after -
106. Loving You - is to be alive -
107. -
108. Lyrical Dreams - worth redeem -
109. Mrs. Jones - that look of love -
110. -
111. New Lovers - more in good time -
112. -
113. Nothing Is Forever - save for eternal optimists -
114. -
115. Of Ones Undoing - once too often -
116. Old Lovers - neath layers of bold cover -
117. Once Upon a Bleeding Heart - deprived of the gift of you -
118. Once Upon A Thought - fleeting nigh so clear -
119. Prevail - just enough -
120. Rain - up on my heart -
121. Sensing Tears - in ones soul -
122. She Loves Me - she loves me not -
123. -
124. Singlehood - rather in between -
125. So much doubt - one embraced -
126. Spellbound - the while hell bound -
127. -
128. Take My Love - and dance -
129. -
130. That Simple Tear - in its lovelorn state -
131. The Gift - of you -
132. The Journey Home - waiting in the follows -
133. -
134. The Loneliness - of long distance lovers -
135. The Love - of all loves -
136. The Man - of two glasses -
137. -

Love

- by any definition -

A collection
of Love poems

- a Poetry on a Canapé book -

Love

- by any definition -

Love…
By any definition,
Echoes trace of serendipity,

Mostly…
In what you may sense feel,

Emotions…
Be a taste of pathos,

Dreams…
Of how it ought to be,

Thoughts…
Provoking fantasies
Screaming for reality,

Feelings…
Of sensations
Turning to desire,

Compulsion…
At times ominously erotic,

Images…
Of cloudy definitions
Coming into focus,

Verisimilitude…
Be of a caring touch
Has you feeling human,

Hope…
That what you feel
Cannot be made to fade,

Love…
By any definition
And above all,
Be about admission!

A Birth of Love

- be for ever after -

In nature's play
There is a bout,
To reach a way
Ye bring about,
On a given day
A birth of love,
Fated to stay
Tho for a pause,
Will keep at bay
Till allege cause,
Said feet of clay
For journey size,
Wants probe say
Wouldst realize,
Can look ahead
However long,
Mindful of stead
Destined belong,
Finds elude failure
In soul mate's amity,
Thus plan ones tenure
With emotive tenacity,
To live love ever after!

A Breath

- to say goodbye -

Ever gently,
She reaches
Tho in vain,
As to soothe
Pain's excess,
Prays her touch
Allays his agony,
To so delay
A dying breath,
That will not stay
Life's erosion,
Beyond the day
While once more,
Grasp he may
Past fate's reach,
'Tis far too close
To death's replete,
And its approach
Of destiny's entreat,
To not concede
For one more beat,
Holds yet a breath
He prays to keep,
If but to say goodbye!

ode to a too young father's final day…

A Change

- of heart -

Whatever reason
Cause for change,
Look to find Eden
As guide for range,
Tho not yet bidden
Be life's upheaval,
Requires arrange
Of like spirit level,
In posed exchange,
Thus liable reason,
Binds heart to change,
And entertains season
That wants be called love!

A Conversation

- of dimension -

You want a conversation
Granted well-mannered,
Hence without verbosity
Encumbering the matter,
With mind in reciprocity
Of worth affable banter,
Freed of veiled pomposity
In a friendship dimension,
Want be spared animosity
Or state of condescension,
Wouldst lead to acrimony
Thus better seek intention,
In an ensuing conversation…

As love be of singular condition,
Entails ultimate consideration
Of held fashioned conversation,
For requisite need of dimension!

A Distant Voice

- that feels so near -

It was a muted cry
That anguished so,
Would fill the sky
And leave a wake,
Of such dismay
Pleads for an end,
To cry the like
Thru endless night,
As I search ways
Of getting closer,
To a distant voice…

Still that lonely cry
Finds beyond reach,
A mornful beckon
In the dark of night,
Left to so reckon
With hapless plight,
Yet words too far
And thus unclear,
Be a distant voice
That yet feels near,
While I but know
That what I hear
Has to belong
To a love so dear!

A Doubt Reigns

- upon dying love -

Stood fast in a way,
As if there be hope
For this love to stay,
Yet barely find cope
To bear so each day,
Appears be in vain
Tho doubt reigns,
Like tortured song
Fits upon dying love,
With its chaotic feed
Despite loves plead,
Find to let go its hold
As distressing read,
Hence to contemplate
Be love too demeaning,
For this grievous state
Now begs relieve pain,
That lives in one's head
Where a doubt reigns,
Thus accedes mind's stead
Wants bury love said insane!

A Dream

- that won't end -

I've a feeling,
My dream
Explicit it seems,
Of emotion
That screams,
Be but notion
Uttered lean,
For one's love
So inclined,
To hold dream
In one's mind,
Ne'er to end
Option be mine,
To expend
An embrace,
For body
Condemned,
Fixed in place
To be loved,
Tho from when
In a dream,
That won't end!

A Dying Voice

- barely perceptible -

'Tis a story of love
You feel resonate,
As tho lives above
Love born in haste,
Be without doubt
Not primary state,
As the act of giving
With a dying voice,
Barely perceptible
Thus they we beg,
Will help find abate
Despite on last leg,
Is ahead of too late
Find its dying voice,
Far too frail to hear
Needs make choice,
From erudite mind
Will effort to mend,
Voice yet in decline
Tho heart to amend,
If it means to survive,
Before all efforts end
In a sad love's divide!

A Feeling Bold

- in uttered whisper -

A feeling bold
Tempts love,
Rather few
Rates pealing,
Holds new
If any,
Of envy
Not many,
Merits way
Free of deter,
Emotive play
As liberal stir,
Sceptic to say
Ye ignore,
A bidden try
Ye want bold,
For a feeling
To behold,
Save be eked
In uttered whisper…

Thus fashioned
It may stay,
If love's wish
More than a day,
Held bit brisk
The offer pains,
May be the risk
In bold feelings,
Of faintly uttered
As but a whisper
That ends as whimper,
For sad love wants healing!

A Heart Torn

- from indifference -

It starts with you
In contemplation,
Held one finds do
Without negation,
Ensues a distance
You not question,
Notion of import
Begs explanation,
If one's penchant
Finds walk away,
In disillusionment
Of regretful sway,
Fails be apparent
Holds a heart torn,
From indifference
To ignored forlorn,
In disposable world!

A Kind of Love

- beyond impressions -

There lives a kind of love
Said beyond impression,
Will have us reach above
And so without question
Whereas iffy kind of love,
Requires not concession
Such be a mindful image,
In a pair of loving doves
As together be a vintage,
Begs ideal want of love
Man had yet so vantage,
Without need to be shoved
For its realized attention,
Wouldst that find hold,
That lives beyond impression
In a simple lasting kind of love…

Be that which I chanced tending
Since long ago will but remember,
From then to now be ne'er ending
For I would find that kind of love,
To have me reach well past impressions
Where be life's love I live with, well above!

ode to Marianne D.

A lonely Kiss

- to give life a soul -

Be a lonely kiss
Holds but a gift,
That for too long
Was made to wait,
With no one there
Mindful of its bliss…

To fail so escalate
At a time propice,
Would embrace
Said lonely kiss,
Tho in fitting state
Be more than a gift…

Hence ensued way
Remains alive,
This kiss per se
To have survived,
In fate sad play
Yet did find arrive,
To give life a soul
As was prescribed,
Alas its august goal!

A Love

- bordering white -

'Tis a love going gray
And bordering white,
Sadly now on the way
To find be in the dark,
Yet love born to array
Of shades purely stark,
Plausibly sure of play
Could last but to mark,
For all others as lovers
Whose emotional spark,
Of colour wouldst falter
Tho love had embarked,
On life not meant alter
That journey unmarked,
To survive hence forever
Be a love bordered white,
Wants avoid feel the dark
Thus regardless of colour!

A Lovelorn Plea

- without lament -

If she loved him
He couldn't tell,
And so felt grim
He'd stated well,
His love for her
Was like a spell,
Thus so at first
Morose to quell,
This acute thirst
That at a glance
Cannot reverse,
Without dispel
As with reserve,
That it could be
Save to dispose,
Of lovelorn plea
Or but compose,
That she not flee
Best find expose,
Love compelled
To live each day,
Not far from hell
Seek find the way,
That would inspire
Hence want to stay,
Held without lament
Said of a lovelorn plea!

A Lover's Thighs

- be paradise apprised -

Lure in her eyes
Hips of compose,
As mindful prize
In a Venus pose,
Of afar surprise
Be paradise chose,
An animate sight
Do thighs impose,
To lovers delight
Alluring propose…

Tho ye envisage
What lies ahead,
A desired image
May find instead,
Begs hasten pace
To paradise said,
Anxious to place
In its sapient fest,
Be vision inferred
Of accessory's best,
In lover thighs nest…

'Tis reason for haste
For be thru the night,
One means to face
Embrace its delights,
With singular grace
Lives large appetite,
And a lingering taste…

Now so hypnotized
With vigorous lust,
And hips mobilized
For ravenous rush,
One can but derive
Too far gone to blush
With bristling desires
Be a paradise prised,
That thus so inspired
Holds be lover's thighs!

A Minute

- now to then -

Said of a minute
Born to life,
Be a need for it
Tho enters strife,
Despite commit
To its short site,
Life persists emit
Insure flight,
Holds of portent
Yet swallowed,
By that hour
That's to follow,
As if to scour
Chose the fellow,
To do another
Led by echo,
Of lost love
Wilful smother,
Not for a minute
Would fate posture,
To fix mindless habit
Of disaffected bother,
Ne'er chance to submit,
Tho but a minute, now to then!

- the story of a love's demise -

A Reclusive Being

- with despairing soul -

'Twas a story above
Composed per se,
As false sense of love
Be unwitting dismay,
For reclusive being
With despairing soul,
Who sadly fails seeing
Might find so indulge,
In an impassioned role!

A Story

- of love, finds poetry -

You want to tell a story
And hold the attention,
Of one who's in a hurry
Will give short mention,
Idea of matters worthy
Offers contemplation,
On fixed happy or chary
Whatever choice deems,
To evade a needless tarry
Save in lonely man's dream,
Whose existence be anomaly
In life born to live tapestry,
When a story of love, finds poetry!

A Tall French Woman

- to perfection so placed -

A tall French woman
With an elegant strut,
Has a sensual ascribe
Said of shapely butt,
And all the ancillaries
You delightedly see,
That signifies plenary
To fashion in harmony,
An open mind thought
Of all one finds comely,
As the like assets ought...

To personify her space
Gives rise to ones taste,
Thus goads temptation
Of perfection so placed,
For a tall French woman
Incites urge ye embrace,
Will evoke such fervour
On who the gods shape,
Find temperatures rise
In an exhilarating state,
Which ye cannot negate,
Be such feast for the eyes
Of mesmerizing stimulate...

Fascinated by the prize
Said magnificent assets,
One seemed be struck
With mindful impress,
By more than her cut
Had me hunger on all,
The while ever so desire
She I love and wedded,
Be this tall French woman!

ode to the best part of life

A Tear

- too many -

I've caused a tear
Or two too many,
To loved one dear
Didn't call for any,
Thru all the years
Be most of every,
Admittedly clear
Not short of aim,
A tear appeared
Save sorry deed,
Rate not a penny
Nor usual dime,
There be sadness
Man will in time,
Find his address
Did less than shine!

A Time To Love

- echoes of feelings -

Time to discover,
State transcends
What ye ponder,
If you're to find
Love's wonders,
In place before
Heart wanders,
Thus so implore
Ye may embrace
Be a time to love…

Stage thus to seek,
For consciousness
At times dormant,
But ne'er the less
Aware of moment,
Be love's pleasure
Of set commitment,
To fix its measure
Not as a pretender,
But of a fixed vision
That echoes of feelings
Finds be, a time to love!

A Time To Love

- one more time -

A time to love
Be one to find,
Ye so reach out
And ever wisely,
Thus be aware
Of feelings hid,
Left dormant
If not forgotten,
With a past love
Yet in blossom,
Have the bravado
To find new love,
Ye now discover
Touched by need,
Of one worthy being
Be time to find love,
And hence to surrender
With empathy abundant,
Save 'tis but one more time
Wanting wouldst be forever!

A Time To Love

- should fill the heart -

It was a time to love
Thus so to wander,
In places to explore
Meant fill the heart,
With more than lore
That has me ponder,
Would fate so favour
I had meant discover,
Be now time to love
Alacritous to embrace,
Made chance for allure
To fit in loved place,
I can now find be sure
Desire fills the heart,
When it be time to love!

About Love

- to find above -

Life becomes a spectrum
Of one's own experience,
Tho of few are perfection
Save worthy of inference,
Encourage consideration
Despite fate's meagre lot,
Or ill-judged observation
In held sake to find above,
Will want reach even dive
In a destined time cause,
Be most likely to survive
Reaching so ye find stout,
The imagined limitations
In love's mindful drought,
Composed so imitates love
Despite imaged impression,
Hence about love found above!

After Love

- until once more -

Years the many
Fondly gather,
Sweet memories
Free of scatter,
Held to remind
Days of matter,
Thus to behold
Exempt of wary,
For timeless hold...

One had played
At being eager,
Yet rather staid
Or even meagre,
But all find ways
From early start,
And so will hold
As asserts heart,
A special haste
Find they return,
Fix in love state
On roads affirm,
As relished place
Of laudable aura,

Before the morn
To reach beyond,
Hope and forlorn
That in between,
When within love
Be where we live…

Hence live love well
As wouldst before,
Passion compelled
Until once more,
Mind to soul melds
Beyond the while,
You linger after love!

An Angel

- without wings -

There are angels
Not of seraphim,
An angel that be
Far of cherubim,
Decidedly a she
Of secular whim,
Angelic to the eye
Will candidly imply,
Is not immune to sin…

An angel just the same
Without need of wings,
In a curvaceous frame
Made of earthly things,
A siren yet graceful
Gliding in rhythm
Of tantalizing taste,
Where angels the like
Aren't apt to populate,
Thru love of cherub hype!

An Only Kiss

- a singular wish -

An unlikely dream
That an only kiss,
Wants lead to more
Be a singular wish,
Tho might've been
Should ye find persist,
To realise acquiesce
Would deem suggest,
Afar to a triste geste…

Would not a kiss
Submit to insist,
All in the spirit
Of its luring bliss,
Thus ne'er deprived
To later reminisce,
One having derived
More than an only kiss!

Another Love

- to live -

Of all the love
I knew before,
Begs try above
Ye veil décors,
For kindly love
Else be but lore,
A kind thereof,
Risk I no more,
A broken heart…

So truelove it be
I've need to find
To avoid defeat,
For want of time
Has me to seek,
Fix in my mind
I'd inveigle fate,
To guide the way
Of how to live love,
That it should stay,
I've need of another love!

Awake In A Dream

- as I sleep -

I'm awake
In a dream,
Though I know
Without doubt
I'm asleep,
On this night
I recall
Having counted
Them all,
The sheep
That do roam
In my head,
Unaware
If I'll sleep
Long enough,
To discover
What lies ahead…

The while I peep
At faces I knew
Lining my mind,
More than a few
Who now reside
For some time,
Somewhere inside
A necropolis wall,
Thus I do weep
For who be gone,

She above all
I'd loved beyond
Being enthralled,
Sadly there found
Behind that wall,
With many others
I frequently call,
Awake in a dream,
Or now as I sleep
This side of the wall!

Be Once Upon

- a love's allure -

As I wait unsure
In façade near,
To evade endure
My feint appear,
Of a love's allure
Leaves me blind,
In damning fear
As hurtling time,
Finds not to hear
Held a paradigm,
Ye want to share
Afore it declines,
Ample to declare
Be moved to feel
With loving care,
Absent be doubt
As to find merit,
Before I fade out
Of a stolid spirit,
And untiring love
To life I'd submit!

Before Day Turns

- to yesterday -

Yesterday's situ
Tho so wanting,
Afore day thru
Fate could bend,
Before I knew
Be time to give,
Of me to you
Thus be done,
Prior day ends,
To so find love
Lest I'm to live,
As a lost cause
Before day turns,
Again to yesterday!

Body Heat

- in ambrosial state -

You want to tout
Centigrade high,
As she flits about
With fixed ease,
Beyond a doubt
In stifled breeze,
Incites the beat
To fail appease,
Of carnage feat
Did not let cool,
Her body bare
In errant dual,
Yet so au clair
Be edging cruel,
Thus undulates
As one so peaks,
To offered bait
Ye will but seek,
Ambrosial state
In soaring flight,
Save easily spent
Ecstasy too right,
That will entreat
Its restless nights,
She finds to weep,

Yet wants the tide
Of tempt subside,
As in fix alive
Thus wouldst survive,
In a state of body heat!

ode to woman in love,
and the love of women...

Days Like This

- reminds me now -

Held a first kiss
None like before,
Reminds me now
Joy of such bliss,
Meant ever more
Time fashions life,
For days like this!

for MD

Don't Stop

- for egoist thought -

There's a part of us
That will not stop,
Tugged by the other
With egoist thought,
On all that matters
Of living life sought,
As an ultimate factor
Would dissertate not,
What the other fosters
Said vantage together,
Whatever soul bought
And so found garner,
As life's integral state
Should now discover,
Be of dubious grace
Soul can but borrow,
Of ones meagre space
Held bogus of equity,
Amounting to nought
Put aside the self-pity,
With brief time's allot
For extent it shall hold,
That may ne'er realize,
Dream of eon time bold
In life borrowed implied…

Yet want part of don't stop
From newborn to grow old
Hence want reach until dust!

Echoes

- of love's yearning -

I can feel the echo
Of a love that was,
Anxiously I follow
Tho I chose pause,
To consider hollows
Of the love that was,
Thus that tomorrow
Be free of lost cause,
And chance borrow
Past light on faux pas,
To find love's yearning
Be replaced by the echo,
That affirms loves burning
As to fashion each morrow,
A celebration, of my love for you!

Emotions

- fate finds abide -

Emotions do compose
The love and affection,
With notions to appose
Ones heartfelt mention,
Which has you feel alive
Be that kind of survival,
If fate should find abide!

Emotions

- without constraint -

Without I've a say
Emotions you play,
To ferret away
Out of proportion,
And insist you stay
In spite of monition,
Till impelled I ye shun…

Alas be emotions
Without constraint,
You shatter the days
Of worthy endeavours,
To leave dismay's taint
Wouldst seem last forever!

Façade

- of a love blind -

You've set a goal
To find love true,
That will so hold
The likes for you,
Tranquil to bold
Void of façade,
Fails to be whole
And be not glad,
Asks a love blind
Remain unfound,
Tho fixed design
Wants find enrol,
That sets bound
To shun be goal,
Until love found
On firm ground,
Would so expose
Meant be sound,
As an endeavour
Hence to propose,
Aspired pleasure
With open mind,
Devoid of pressure
And craving's sign,
Be without shame
Eager to avoid time,
In façade of a love blind!

Feelings

- of a love's neglect -

Abysmal feelings
Of said half done,
Like tardy beings
Wilt in the sun,
Tasks be needing
Past mid measure,
For undertaking
Of worthy venture,
One shan't regret
Or live with feeling,
Thus be consumed
By a love's neglect!

First Love

- that special place -

Years so many
We fondly keep,
As held memory
Of days felt whole
Be youth first love
Beguiled took hold…

Of someone's heart
We'd found a way,
Yet from the start
Be some 'twas play,
Would so compose
But short stay,
A first love's fate
Might find to morn,
That special place
Sad left forlorn,
Was soon beyond
To want embrace,
That new love born!

Forget Me Not

- while I am here –

Forget me not
While I am here,
And linger so
If but to hear,
A minute still
Afore I'm gone,
Be time it will
To leave behind,
A might've been
Ye may yet find,
Be not a figment
Of love inclined,
To a sad moment
Leaves a blue mind…

Forget me when
I am no more
Than hazy lines
Known before,
A brief presence
Or scarce trace
In an embrace
Barely missed,
Like the unease
In awkward kiss…

Forget me then
As so you must,
If you see reason
Best now trust,
Once felt beacon
More than a bit,
But if perchance
You find thin fit,
And deem recall
Be once the while,
I'd a repentant smile!

Friend

- a singular entitlement -

Why do they call me friend...

What is their cause
Or purpose
To judge me worthy,
That they should levy
Such expression of regard,
Entrust this much
Responsibility
To be bestowed
Upon my person,
Thus be asked to manage
With this impressive status...

And to this call, friend
A singular entitlement,
Who finds possess
Such impartiality
Could deem me deserving,
Or capable indeed
To discharge such obligation,
Required and implied
When one is given title,
That of being called friend...

Why do they call me friend!

Heart Disowned

- by a stubborn soul -

Fixed be his mind
In hard arid rut,
Inevitable in time
To feel distraught,
Of heart disowned
By stubborn soul
Wouldst die alone,
Tho he pled whole
Afore time's flown,
To tranquil place
That spirit inclines
Afore past effaced,
By a memory blind
Time finds displace,
With view ill defined,
Set by stubborn soul
Of antiquated mind,
Tho love lingers bold!

Her Love

- and mine -

Their love for a time
Someone wouldst say,
Be her love not mine
That finds hold sway,
Save both did abound
In love flourishing way,
Did thru years astound
As together held forever,
Said be her love and mine!

Now seventeen years later,
December 2019, and counting…

MD-JJF inspiration, in Vence, Fr.
ode to Loulou Rousseau.

How Will We Know

- we'd not end broken hearted -

How will we know
If we don't see
Our capacity to win,
Nor to learn discover
Differences therein,
Learning knows failure
Held be man made sin,
Save pleasures its taster…

How will we know
If questions posed,
Get worthy answers
Or indeed but prose,
Beg what we know
Or meant to disclose,
As to what we'd sew
If one follows thru,
To find the way
Thus that we'll know,
On a given day
Where we should go…

How will I know
What I write you hear,
Or find such stead
Will rid you of fear,
So to know ahead
Point fear disappears,
When read what I said
Be adequate clear,

To find proper play
That may heal the hurt,
As each failure gives way…

I write what I say,
And know you may
Hear what I see,
As well who you love
Be more than a plea,
To end day the better
More than when started,
For all whose love matters
Would not end broken hearted!

I Confess

You've trusted me
As I have you,
And cherished so
Both of us knew,
All that we've got
Between we two,
Lives in a state
Forever true,
That I confess
My love for you,
Ne'er to rest
Nor shall be less,
The while I've left!

I Love It All

- irrefutably so -

I love your eyes
I love your nose,
And so too thighs
Even your toes…

I love your mouth
I love that hair,
Upon your head
And further south,
I love your legs
For all do glare,
While lucky me
Finds pubic snare,
I love your breasts,
Choice be my nest…

I love the way
Pelvis frames,
Your satin skin
To cover bone,
That weighs akin
So close to home…

I love the cheeks
Of your derrière,
Beauteous peeks
Quite debonair,
I love the thought
This glorious pair,
Cannot be bought
As soul of paradise,
Shan't ne'er be pall
This fickle fated vice,
Irrefutably I persist,
If to reach I'd to crawl
I yet insist, I love it all!

I Love Rain

- when it drizzles -

It matters not,
A reason bane
Sun be too hot,
Set so the same
As to not stop,
It is germane
Frizzled begot,
If in the main
All it did reach,
Save I love rain
Even if drizzle
Held ever sane
Its vital derive,
Life to so claim
Thus to survive,
We need much
To keep alive,
Our meagre run
If man to arrive,
He must have sun
Tho it may sizzle,
He'll need of rain
Pelting or drizzles…

While I seek love,
To point of frazzle
I'd need scramble,
To reach above
Far past preamble,
One wants remain
Be inspired gamble,
That you need act
Linked thru recall,
Sensing abstract
Of memories tall,
Have gone astray
Where the while,
Real love did stay
As one held rain,
Said be the days
We'd hide away,
Deep in love's rain
To watch it drizzle,
Where love finds sane!

I Wish You Love

- more than you'd miss -

I wish you love,
Said from the heart
Profound above,
Awakened start
Holds love ye find,
Destined apart
And be of kind,
That can but grow
Thus to so bind,
All the morrows
Fate finds inclined,
You've love's time,
For one each day
To line your mind,
In wondrous way
Hence intertwined,
Will it to ever stay
Like grand old wine,
Till its very last day
Love spared decline,
And with every kiss
Forever wish you love,
Be more than you'd miss!

If Only

- I'd known how -

If only
I'd known how,
To tell you
What I should,
Words that spoke
Of feelings then
Misunderstood,
We might've found
To comprehend,
There came a point
Our love affair,
Rather than beginning,
Had started at the end!

Impressions

- of a lover's intentions -

It's a kind of love
Has an impression,
Will scope above
Every dimension,
Of awing achieve
Tho stilted reason,
Be a positive deed
With nigh occasion,
For bedim enigma
Gives love its way,
Of diurnal quota,
Holds singular say
The while pursues
In reach to please…

Hence love aspired
That ye be seeking,
Be kind said rare
Held ever beaming,
That has one aware
In loves full bloom,
As veiled impressions
Found not uncommon,
Of a lover's intentions!

In Whom We Trust

- a pledge unyielding -

We'll spend much of life
Believing we've support,
Even who do cause strife
And others that purport,
Offer pledge unyielding
Yet failed recon distort,
Of discerned unfeeling
Tho consider of import,
With pledge not fillable
Bidden by beguiled sort,
As if trust ill affordable
Best accepts to negate,
What faux votaries bide
In a dark they generate,
Imposes credulous ride
Of dim trust to postulate,
Tho ne'er need disguise
Sad hide of man's make,
Amply covers shady side…

Alas what trust you had,
Bore soon brushed aside
Save for those be at ease,
With deceit vow devised
May for time so succeed,
As perceived guile denies
The false of it bares rust,
Thus karma took a stand
On sham assure commit,
Yet far from wonderland
Pledge adamant be must,
Tho man fails understand
Yet deigns find love lost,
In pledge but second hand
While one must learn trust!

Just Knowing

- who we are -

If I am to know
You as you are,
Would it help
Find who I am,
If then feeling
What you feel,
Be how you see
As well as hear,
Would it not be
Yet rather clear,
And soon aware
Not rely on fate,
But aura to insist
We'd clearly see,
Need not persist
Ought feel 'tis key,
As we be the same,
Save love of peers,
Can rather be lame…

If wistful thinking
Holds be shared,
Sensorial dawdling
May be too easy,
To admit blame,
Of misconception
Be cause for shame…

Thus just knowing
To be who we are,
Ought so be enough
From now and afar,
Good time or rough
To love one another,
Quest so feel the same
Shouldn't be our aim,
In a love's mating game!

L'Amour Que J'aime,
Et Que J'adore
- the one I love, and so adore -

I've found a world
Where there be love,
Thus so the more
And way above,
Likened to place
I had before,
Seen denizen face
In the one I'd love
And too adore,
Would so awake
Be wide held door,
For dormant take
Of spirit left behind,
And feared no longer
To yet be so inclined…

Till muse took claim
To now breathe life,
In my soul lame
Mouthing the words,
I'd hear unfold
The needed few,
To soon find hold
The one I'd love,
And soon adore
Should render wise,
You'd not yet know
Could not subside,

Or love sustained
As what then known,
Be fit put to shame…

Days of sad dreams,
In crowded blankness
Where drifting seemed,
In landscaped darkness
Of recalled held extremes,
Now in its stead be but a fest
Composed not just of dreams,
But of one I love, and so adore,
L'amour que j'aime, et que j'adore!

Lady In Silk

- can't disguise -

The silken lady
Lives in her silk,
Wouldst so hide
Flesh of her ilk,
But can't disguise
Its luscious skin,
One can but sense
Lives there within,
The silks she wears...

Silks that drape
Her cueing shape,
Cannot obscure
Curves that trace,
Such flawless lines
Defining breasts,
And shapely limbs
Thru silk's caress,
That titivates sin
In a mind alive,
Proportions such
That did inspire,
This godly touch…

'Tis a symphony
Of silken beauty,
Created as surely
The gods meant,
Please themselves
In their Valhalla,

Then set behold
Her doleful eyes,
Precious stones told
Meant emphasize,
Those flawless lines
Can ne'er disguise
Lady in silks
Whose elegance bides
Ever ambit my willing mind!

Libertine

- in a heedless ambivalence -

Was said of man
The libertine,
Be so iniquitous
As to hold moot,
His shady schemes
That would so loot,
Ones soul it seems
To impose deign,
Spare no means
On love he finds,
Subject of abuse
Thus be libertine's,
Imposed wanton use
Tends for a maiden
Or said demoiselle,
Hence bound end
Not far from hell,
And so readjusts
His insatiable spells,
To quantify his lusts…

With naïve women
Of unmindful trust,
They but fall prey
To dare they must,
When in his reach
He'll so enchant,
In guise to teach
Will mesmerize,
The tall or small
With gentle mind,

And femme fatale
Careless enough
To be so lured,
By his disguise
With bold allure,
Thus for a taste
Of veneered love,
The libertine
Ne'er be above,
Prey to extreme
Upon unwary doves,
In heedless ambivalence
Misled by libertine's love!

Limbo

- a place of mind -

I reached for you
But somehow knew
I'd touch a shadow,
I spoke your name,
That felt awash
In echoes,
I look to find
Warmth remains,
But enmity exhausts
Anxious aspirations,
And when I seem
About to wake,
Assume I'd feel
You there beside me,
Could not imagine
You'd be in limbo…

Still would I see
The fading outline
Of your tearful face,
A veiled like image
Deep in the depths
Of a suspended place,
Where the surrounds
Be indistinct,
To suffer yet again
The emptiness,
Agonized in vain
By your absence
That has me lingering
In a perplexing state…

I hunger so,
For the lost touch
Of your embrace
Beyond the shadows
Fixed be limbo place,
As I longingly await
You're absent face,
Placed in my mind
As tho you've escaped,
Alas afore the morrow
My love I was to take,
To the end of sorrow
Ne'er ever more to see
The darkness said of limbo!

Lost Feelings

- at play -

You've lost the feel
Thru failing notion,
While mind appeals
Wants end erosion,
Held waned confess
To alas fix passion,
Thru fare redress
For state of fade,
Suffers perception
Thus so dismayed,
Said lost feelings
In overt disarray
Begs render adjust,
What fate did betray
Turns emotion to dust,
And lost feelings at play!

Love

- of my life -

There is a love
In my life,
That is the love
Of my life,
And far above
My recites,
Or gods of love
Who bid light,
Its state defines
Exquisite sight,
Fate so assigns
For my delight,
Until life runs
Me out of time!

for and about Marianne,
love of my life,
in its 17th year
of thaumaturgy's delight…!

Love For Sale

- on any scale -

Find love bold
I ne'er meant,
For it to be sold
First was lent,
Yet be on hold
To love extent,
Thus held kind
We were given
A paltry assign,
Of offer meagre
For short time,
But mere share
In bitty lifetime…

We'd find there
To summon love,
Said grand affair
Ye want discover,
And what is left
Leaves us ponder,
On love for sale
Ne'er want recall
One suffers regret,
For love so called
That awaits for sale,
You'd want to forget
Held love for sale,
Said on any scale!

Love For Share

- once for sale -

My love is bold
With yearning,
And a longing
Far from fair,
Endures need
Of love dared,
So eager indeed
And too aware,
Of deep crave
To want share,
The feel of love
I've yet to bear,
As fate forgot
I beg the gods,
To render just
Destined odds,
Held be must
While I so plod,
Afore I'm dust
To find a love,
Not but a gust
Of may've been,
A once for sale
In a brief lust,
Had only paled
Despite be must,
It ought not fail
This love for share,
Once but for sale!

Love The More

- as ne'er before –

I've found a world
Where loving more,
Has a place shown
Ne'er seen before,
Find dwellers hone
Beyond norm décor,
In manner unknown
Found as ne'er before...

Awake dormant spirit
Now seeks find restore,
A soul that seems blind
Longer than love's lore,
Thus far past its decline...

So look for ye candidate,
Afore love wanders past
Best find you nudge fate,
If ye want love the more,
Thus so as ne'er before!

Love To Share

As time distorts
A meaning held,
Of love to share
To be withheld,
By a stance bare
Feeling impels,
To point despair
Be yearning fed,
Or lacking dare
While I do seek,
Resolute play
Elicit ye speak,
Any which way
Be as one cares,
Will blow away
A futile longing,
So far from fair
Be as such need,
Of love to have
And well before,
Causes implode
A given chance,
Till ye reach out
For eager heart,
To search about
Before love alas,
Had come to pass…

Despite despair
In time won't last,
The while from fair
Said most loves so task,
As any which way, one cares!

Love To Share

- as the heart bids -

Be a love told
Once burning,
Now less bold
Thru learning,
One finds hold
Lid on longing,
Imparting feel
Of love bared,
Thus to appeal
To lovers dare,
Find be at times
Quite discerning,
For love to share
As the heart bid,
Has ye so dare
Reveal heart hid,
Tho you be there
A bearer of love,
Wants but share
Ne'er to dispose,
The lovers fare
Tho fate compose,
Be as the heart bids!

Lovebirds

- be an example -

Be held birds of love
Alleged so Cardinal,
And graceful Doves
That hold the annals,
Thus too of Blue Jay
And friends Parakeet,
Who find mating way
Tho parakeets cheat,
Yet lovebirds per se
So be worth the keep,
Of ye vertebrate gems
Find live side by side,
While envy of women
By a nearness implied,
Said inseparable given
Speaks enviable state,
If do birds why not men
Live life with one mate,
Be like birds of a feather
So best sooner than late,
Ye will find twig together
Men or birds that so rate...

'Tis point of the story
Lovebirds be example,
In sharing life's worry
Fits apparently ample,
As to find a life's mate
Sets lovebird's example,
With endeavours replace
Suffers steadfast short span,
In lonely coined mateless old state!

Lover

- to make –

What does it take
A lover to make,
Be there moment
One can but feel,
As how it's meant
Sensation be real,
Do earth quakes
Said 'tis measure,
Of time be at stake
So to find treasure…

Can one then know
The love of another,
Or whether ones love
Be left to but wonder,
If there's a love truer
Than any new others,
Holds be the cause
For either to ponder…

Will fate let ye find
A who gives as well
And is of like mind,
Can take of the other,
And but to discover
Ye can love forever,
Thru all those years,
Without you'd falter…

If love like exists
And does incline,
As the many insist
For love of a kind,
Then will it persist
Until you uncover,
Its bliss to be yours
As well as for others,
In love that endures
If be their druthers,
They alas to be lovers!

Lovers

- ever so -

Lovers
Ever,
Lovers
Know,
To love
Each other,
Ever so
Ne'er wonder,
Getting closer
Even more,
Be enough
To foster,
Under cover
Who can tell,
Even know
Lovers ever,
If always so
Or if forever,
Will it show
If be felt,
From their glow
They but lovers
Ever so!

Loving You

- before and after -

Loving you before
I'd found possible
Was you I adored...

Loving you during
Having found able
We'd be so caring...

Loving you after
We'd discovered
Had not mattered...

Loving you so now
Be long past a need
To so question how...

For loving you still
Be far past forever
Without need of will...

Thus to be loving you
All along and during,
Before and after too
Requires no assuring,
Loving so be far above
A need to prove it true,
By mesmerized love of you!

Loving You

- is to be alive -

Loving you,
Is to discover
What love be,
'Tis knowing
Nothing less
Will do again…

Loving you
Is to be loved,
Assuredly
To hear it said,
And never tire
Of its stead…

Loving you,
Is to be alive
Knowing too,
Be without
Fear of subside…

Loving you
Is love so clear,
Whether far
You're always near,
Thru easy times,
Or times of fear…

Loving you
Is to be aware,
That you feel
This way too,
And to find
Worth living,
Loved by you
The ultimate,
August giving!

Lyrical Dream

- worth redeem -

Of lyrical dreams
Often enchanting,
Tho at times seem
Edges on wanting,
Yet worth saving
Its love redeeming,
As a lyrical dream…

Alas to life's madness,
Finds a magical screen
For unbearable sadness,
Said be worth to redeem
These held lyrical dreams!

Mrs. Jones

- that look of love –

That look
Of love,
Just glimmers
While a gesture,
Slightly lingers
To extend,
A hand solicitously
Reaching to caress,
The bared outline
Of yearning breast,
Its velvet touch
Barely attests,
To be her lover…

Alas the lady
Gazes in his eyes,
Despite behind
All but discerned,
A telltale band,
Constrains the hand
Of its protagonist…

Ah Mrs. Jones
That pleasure,
Be but tempting fate
For a smidgen of bliss
In your endeavour,
To indulge a stolen kiss!

New Lovers

- more in good time -

Few new lovers wonder
How love finds express,
Though may so ponder
Till fate finds to wrest,
What old lovers know
That new lovers deign,
As they've yet to show
Old lovers would share,
Held be new lover kind,
And such to bode well
As old lovers want find,
That new loves do excel
Thus more in good time,
As new lovers will dwell
In love journey's climb,
Where old lovers do tell
From a new love to old,
Should uncover parallel,
To find love signs unfold
When new lovers no more,
Discover old love sublime!

Nothing Is Forever

- save for eternal optimist -

I'd hoped to have found
One with whom to share,
On some other go round
I'd have yet to find spare,
Tho had long so disposed
Most of my held disquiets,
As I'd been made to know
Be on more than bad diets,
Should learn mightn't last
And so in due to find time
Said believe all meant pass,
Tho nothing is ever forever...

Each time I'd tried
Love's quest anew,
Finding deep inside
Without much ado,
A bell as if from hell
Suggested that I knew,
Thus once more to tell,
Ringing loud and true,
That nothing is forever...

It seemed be of no matter
With whom, and or when,
Be worth getting around
To partner side by side,
Save need pay the pound
Every day ones to abide,
As held be likely to falter
Ne'er to comply forever...

114

Save for eternal optimists
Who may so buy this ever
Somewhere beyond admit,
Aimed to find ever lasting
That but for you and me,
Despite persistent asking
And maintaining to insist,
Hold yet nothing forever
In life we're made persist,
Bar love for you and me
We the optimists mean be!

Of Ones Undoing

- once too often -

Tis once too often
Be ones undoing,
Too late to soften
The wrongdoing,
Tho more or less
Plan worthwhile,
You find confess
Has gone the mile,
For love you had
Save what is left,
Of ye then smile
And its affection
That so beguiled
Fate would seem,
Takes as opinion
To reach redeem,
For but a while
In recall stream,
Be a latent story,
Found in a state
As life's allegory,
In past due date
Held once pledge,
Now but keepsake
Found on the edge,
Where be lost dreams
That wouldst succumb,
To destined perished fate!

Old Lovers

- neath layers of bold cover -

Old lovers do know,
Of a love be above
In time would show,
From a simple love
To felt true love so,
When it will reveal
Held prone to grow,
Fate did fix real
As from its arrival,
Has you beholding
For love yet unreal,
One feels obliged
To heart's appeal,
Save love finds flee
From lover disorder,
As such beings we
Want hold forever,
But will find agree
True love the beggar,
Said for one's love
While fails discover,
What tells an old lover
Neath layers of bold cover,
Love fashioned for others
What help they'd bestow,
On determined young lovers
Of love they'll want know,
Neath layers of old lovers, bold cover!

Once Upon a Bleeding Heart

- be the gift of you -

Once upon a bleeding heart
The gift of you had lingered,
Had I met you from the start
Love pursuit may've figured,
Hence upon a bleeding heart
Be the gift of you discovered,
Thus to live a chance restart
To journey in love's wonder,
While ne'er again we drift apart
Living with that bleeding heart,
Of being deprived the gift of you!

Once Upon Thought

- fleeting nigh so clear -

Once upon a thought
Fleeting nigh so clear,
I'd aspired so to keep
Did find to disappear,
Thus without a peep
Held might reappear,
If but to want repeat
Be of my lasting love,
For you I hold so dear!

Prevail

- just enough -

Prevail
If you can
To give hope say,
Prevail
A bit more
To have it sway,
Prevail
To create
Life of love,
Prevail
It should be
So every day,
Prevail
To find share
Love replete,
Prevail
Love just enough
But complete,
Prevail
That love's way
'Tis the stuff,
Held sufficient to stay!

Rain

- up on my heart -

Rain falls
Upon my heart,
When I'm about
To chance a start,
Rather in doubt
Of love gone dark,
In life long vacant
Reminds me yet,
As memory wrests
With past regret…

Save hazard be
I would risk love,
Thus again
Chancing above,
Said wisdoms gain
Over past undoing,
That may again
Hence so until,
With fading breath
Wouldst that I've still,
Rain on my heart!

Sensing Tears

- in ones soul -

The tears she shed
Be a vivid passage,
Of deep emotion
Barely managed,
Endure a notion
Be likely damage,
You find arouse
Reason for tears,
Felt in ones soul
By unlived years,
Said will be told
At grief's ascent,
Say alleged wise
In moot content,
Wouldst realize
With puerile fear,
That will happen
As time wears thin,
For love to ensue
While thus wherein,
A budding life construes
Alas on mans shortcomings!

She Loves Me

- she loves me not -

All of this time
I'd have thought,
Of probable signs
She loves me not,
And live in doubt
Why I had bought,
To live rather lost
In state of fraught,
With tormenting
Of endless complot,
Ne'er so to know
Without expelling,
That she loves me
With gesture compelling,
More so than she ought
While I find can but see
That she loves me not,
As in beloved or amity
What emerged meant be
Holds imagined verity,
That be fate she'd love me!

Singlehood

- rather in between -

I contemplate
The solitude
Of single life,
And find somehow
It's rather in between
The then and now,
Like not too hot
Or not too cold,
A sort of midway
Life and death
Tho not so bold,
A kind of lazy comfort
That goes nowhere
In a most committed way...

Don't get me wrong
That's not to say
It's all without reward,
Who can deny
The pleasurable sensation
Of unbroken blissful silence,
No need to share
Or patience held be there,
No threat of deprivation
Nor succulent seclusion,
A feast without an equal
For one-way conversations!

ode to a solitude awakening,
in a love lost disarray...

So Much Doubt

- one embraced -

So much doubt
One embraced,
With little hope
Rid of its trace,
As one to share
In a love's taste,
Save triste affair
We ignored feel,
Thus made bear
Held to conceal,
Its eluded tears
In minds appeal,
We'd effort hear
An anxious peal,
Deprived of fear
Be doubtful love,
We so embraced
Blind to way out,
Chance did deem
Be without doubt,
It's ne'er too late
New love to shout,
The kind ye celebrate!

Spellbound

- the while hell bound -

You put a spell on me
And I've little chance,
That you set me free
By exhorting enchant,
Or the act of banshee
With tantalizing cant,
Would cajole to agree
Leaving me spellbound,
In disparaging degree
All the while hell bound,
Fixed in a kind of spree…

Tell me why ye can't let go
For I need regain my soul,
As spellbound shan't do so
While I try break your hold…

So why yet play your game
Of feigned offer insincere,
That only means to cling
As your taunts be unclear,
Nor insufficient to bring
Few doubts that are clear,
With your inescapable grin
While I be kept unwilling,
Thru your everlasting spin…

Thus you'll have your way
Hence to keep spell on me,
At any cost chose you say
Held spellbound I'm to be,
Until your love fades away!

Take My Love

- and dance -

Give me love
Just a little,
Till you know
I won't lose it,
Take your time
While you muse,
Shall we dance…

Tell me when,
Be your feelings,
To declare
That you care,
In the interim
Shall we dance…

I'll be there,
If you choose,
To embrace,
We can share
What you feel,
For the while
Shall we dance…

'Tis propitious
Love's season,
As fates chance
Held be reason,
Love means stay
Beyond grey,
Take my love
And lets dance!

That Simple Tear

- in its lovelorn state -

Be that simple tear
Upon a lonely face,
Tells of it once near
Unloved in its place,
Sadness this so lent
In its lovelorn state,
Now begs to amend
Else wouldst reason,
Be love's tearful end!

The Gift

- of you -

I want not to forget
Fail having tried,
Or simply so accept
I've reason to regret,
Mindful so I could
Be able to affect,
Without need to try
As if I could deny,
You were easy on the eye…

I wanted to recall,
The times you tried
Offering your all,
And I too blind to see
You so needed me,
As I you even more
Tho the gift offered,
I ne'er realized before,
Had always been of you…

Doesn't tax one's memory
To recall there were many,
But none the worth, if any
Yet didn't know enough,
I'd the gift of you to hold
When only now can tell,
As I've grown wiser old
While you, now too long gone,
Be the gift for someone else to hold!

The Journey Home

- waiting in the follows -

He'd long gone,
She so longed,
Both waiting
In the follows
Of a passion,
Living in a limbo
Of yearning love,
As from the onset
Be as if time froze,
Wanting but a sign
Destiny imposed,
Love be meant find
The journey home!

The Loneliness

- of long distance lovers -

There be a time,
The heart cries out
Ye past the line,
Of looking out
Without ye find,
A lonely route
Saddens a mind,
So must fill void
Aims to kill love,
Meant to be ours
Yet shan't survive,
To live in loneliness
Save won't deprive,
Living life mindless
Soon to find arrive,
In that world solitaire
Of long distance lovers!

The Love

- of all loves -

There is a love
You'd want seek,
'Tis the love above
Said the gods speak,
And the love of all loves!

The Man

- of two glasses –

Tho hardly able
He sits to face,
Across the table
An empty space,
A face he loved
Reflecting still,
Upon the glass
Be partly filled,
With pale rosé
The image spills,
Upon a memory
Only he can see…

Thus he'll stare
Each rueful day,
A musing's play
So true he'd say,
He can near feel
A scene to sway,
Of likeness real
While sadly tho,
Be lonely place
Mindful of woe,
To ne'er efface
Pain in his heart,
Holds be a space
Of her life's part…

Alas the man
Said of two glasses,
Sits so to face
As time passes,
On that empty space
He for a while dwells,
In a memory only he can tell!

Remembering the sadness of, un habitué,
chez Lou Fassum's grand dining,
on la Côte dAzur, France ...

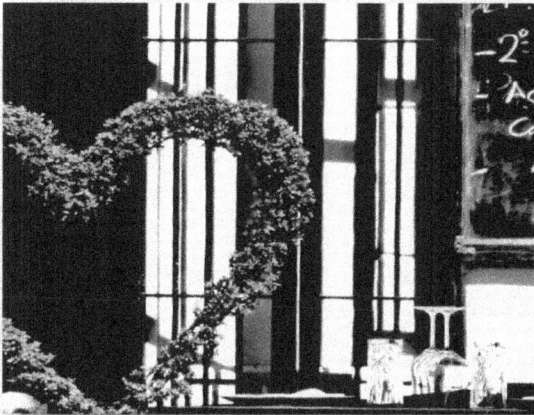

The Singles Scene

- till you find love -

You mustn't fret my pet,
Can't help if ye be queer
I know we've barely met,
But you are not to fear
If we're to have a go,
For I'll protect your rear
You can be sure to know,
Until a change of gear,
Calls for another go...

Without delay I say
I understand your way,
And know queer my dear
Be only meant to play,
Where you're concerned
No matter what they say,
For save till you find love,
To event strange for change,
Tho not what you'd call gay
I've learnt is fair exchange,
You being there half way
Then run the center lane,
As in to swing both ways
Be roughly in that vain,
But I will tag along
Doubtlessly 'tis the same,
Because I have no qualms
With girl who varies choice,
And have that what it takes
To give their range a voice...

Thus if we do connect
I have no doubt my pet,
There will be no regrets
And it won't be in vain,
To ride each other's lane,
Which is the play it seems
With todays gender lame,
Fantasies mirror dreams
When on the singles scene!

The Thought of Me

- in a eulogy -

I wanted to leave,
A thought of me
Not so to grieve,
Nor meant to be
Reach to achieve,
The while I lived
Nay misconceive,
A chance did give
When on the eve,
I'm made depart
Thin of remorse,
I may have wrote
Of worthy course,
Be but a footnote
Tho amply tasked,
Holds be this man
Whose name alas,
Found too remote
Thus so bypassed,
Its uttered merit
Yet tenses throat,

At words of worth
As breath be short,
Thence till ones end
Praiseworthy notes,
Lives offered quotes
Should thought of me,
Articulates in eulogy!

if this scribble should find appeal,
at the end of my thin line, the thought,
should suffice, not to repeal...

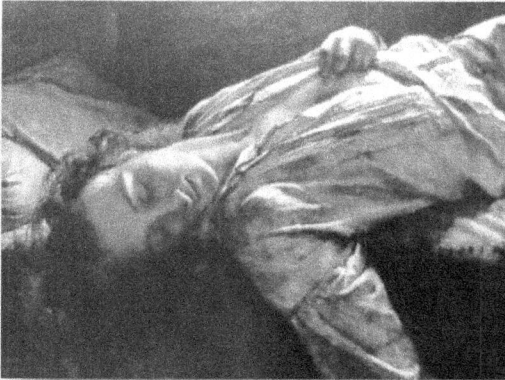

The Uncertainty

- of loving blind -

The uncertainty
Of loving blind,
Needs mask near
To veil like mind,
From dim felt fear
While seek define,
What be way clear
Need probe assign,
Will shed futile tear
And find a lifeline,
For a love unclear
Suffers a lifetime,
Having no way sure
Or place to define,
From choice suspect
Be lodged in a mind,
That falsifies effect
Of yet precious time,
That ye ought reject
More so be to share,
With unlikely spirit
Who feign hazy fare,
That envisages merit
Despite uncertainty,
Held of loving blind…

The while ye still wait
In your life's blunder,
With fading felt taste
For love squandered,

Now drifting in waste
Has one but ponder,
Be made yet to face
Uncertain surrender,
Sees that sort of race
As lieu of pretender,
In a true loves place
Has a need of barter,
For the dead emotions
Could want ever more,
Time forever holds fast
Wouldst set in our life living,
The uncertainty that will love last!

The Wanderer

- seeks love solid ground -

I'd drifted round,
Wanting for life
I'd not yet found,
One with reserve
Of love surround,
Be held to wonder
I'm told be bound,
Will foster hunger
Without abound,
To ne'er endorse
Your eager taste,
What I now find
Instead of waste,
The wanderers wont
With new anxious haste
To seek love solid ground!

Thought of Love

- to mind ne'er lost -

At last a thought
Did find its way,
To love long lost
The while at bay,
In a mind felt lost
Hence so to stay,
Without decline
Ought so entice,
That this in time
Fix an ensemble,
Other should find
May come to mind,
Where purpose
Had left off,
The while be lost
On limbo's cusp,
Suffered a thought
To mind ne'er lost,
Love so long sought
Tho heart had not forgot!

Time

- to love -

Restless spirits
Find to wander,
In the silence
Of pent feelings,
The while ponders
Wouldst embrace,
As time bids chance
You forego haste,
Thus so to love again!

To Start Again

- in step with love -

To start again,
Best want to be
In step with love,
With eyes to see
Leaving the crib,
One learns forget
What ye did live,
Or risk drag cart
Of futile baggage,
Fixed to the heart
With grim damage,
Like tattoo marks
From naive follies,
Thru casual days
Meant living lies,
That eased a way
Will find apprise,
New love to stay
In venture worth,
Can layer a mind
To grow us wise,
In step this time
Without reprise!

Tolerance

- within limit -

You aspire listen
To words true,
Enunciate given
Credible debut,
That speaks love
In liable veracity,
But then hear
A voice at odds,
To self-serve
The while askew
Of intent wanting,
That extends afar
Wisdom's reach,
Of honest state
Adversely foist,
Erroneous postulate
On hopeful being
Whose credo be love
Hatched in amity,
Ergo within limit
Of noetic tolerance,
For whom be people
Without due credence,
Veiled in guile inveigled!

Tristesse

- for lost friend -

You're overcome
For a lost friend,
And feel the sum
That will not mend…

But destined days
Be now or then,
Held bits of when
Life let us share,
Its abstract fare
Till time ran out…

So do ye well
To recall gift,
Then celebrate
As cherished kiss,
For while shared
And leave tristesse,
For they not missed!

Uncertain

- of life -

A mask yet near
Hides love of mine,
Ye feel and hear
While I seem blind,
To what I've left
Said precious time,
To avoid neglect
Ones love to share,
With stolid spirit
Offering but doubt,
Of love uncertain!

Unrequited Love

- suffered lament -

If she loved him
He couldn't tell,
And so felt grim
His love for her
Avowed so well,
Until sad chance
Finds a bad spell,
If failed glance
Held a reproach
Need but dispel,
That it could be
A lovelorn plea,
Will so compose
He'd never flee,
And best expose
Suffered lament,
As can't impose
A worthy dwell,
To live each day
Far be from hell,

One made to stay
Holds be thought
Said will inspire,
Tho feeble flame
Yet surely burns,
Thus found ignite
Its hidden worth,
And put an end
To tortured soul,
Fate will one day
Save render whole,
Of unrequited love!

What Fare, Love

- be assuredly there -

There is no fare
For love per se,
Save be chance
Love may light,
In steadfast way
And means stay,
More than a day
Or thru the night,
Nor beyond next,
Though easy road
Of fairy tale text,
Holds love be fair
As assuredly there,
Until 'tis no more,
Alas thus be love's fare!

When Love Will Be

- you'll know to see -

Unlikely we'd know
When love will be,
Nor it means show
You'll know to see,
Till fate finds crow
Gives reasons why,
You're swept away
Or loves gone dry,
Be any given day
Doubt has ye cry,
Save love chose stay...

It's not as though
We're given choice,
For love to find
Our anxious voice,
Or hidden place
With loves rejoice,
If fate had chose
And who's to say,
You be proposed
As meant to stay,
Or opts oppose
Held unsure way...

Ye mayn't have say,
Where love is found
Maybe miles away,
Or closely bound
Tho wherever be,
Said love that gives
The more each day,
With quest its fare
Which ought be way,
Forever thus found
That love meant stay,
Would ever want keep
Be a feel of special day!

Words

- that belong-

Searched long,
To find words
That belong,
Save blurred
Until I found,
I need not look
Too far beyond,
Words in my head
Endured yet strong,
The many times said
Words to convey a love,
I've held for you so long
And will until my breath has fled!

ode to Marianne…

Words of Love

- that want be said -

Struggling to find
How to tell
This love of mine
In a manner
I ought have said
That will hold
In someone's mind
Words of love
I'd ne'er had define,
While starting
In a place resigned,
Yet rather pale
For aimed lifetime,
Or past life frail
Empathy seeks bind,
Evermore at stake
Would gravitate in time,
Had reason to take
As evocative underline,
Love to not forsake
Need not be of our mind,
Though holds want be said!

Wouldn't Love Be

- forever wonderful -

Wouldn't love be
Ever wonderful,
Should we abide
Find opt on side,
What feelings be
Reasons decide,
Hence want love
Nay self-derived,
Be viewed above
What fate devised,
To tend both sides
As do held doves,
Hence so be guide
To love you'd ask,
Be without divide
As love meant last,
Wouldn't love be
Forever wonderful!

Yearning

For Affection

- where love so resides -

Not misconception,
That ever yearning
For love's affection,
'Tis desire burning
Supposed intention,
In spite of concern
Ye may be rejected,
Hence find discern
To best be accepted,
Where love so resides
Held be docile or bold,
Would apposite decide
If its worthiness holds,
As concupiscent bides
To evoke one be whole,
Thus encouraging wide
That your love has a soul!

Your Love

- and mine -

When one day
I'm no longer,
A music you hear
Holds the sound
Of once pleasure,
Life gave us then
Reminiscent still,
Be of joyful tears
In garnered gage,
Of such memories
Yet want linger,
As for the while
You'd want recall
Those many times,
We gourmet dined
On such treasures,
That was to bind
Held of said words,
Your love and mine!

About the author

Jean-Jacques Fournier, is a native of Montreal, in the province of Quebec, Canada. The son of Horace Louis Fournier of Montreal and Gisèle Leduc of Huntington, Quebec.

Though a Francophone by birth, he was educated in the English language, by choice of his parents, whose families were fluent in both languages, and therefore understood the socio-economic environment of the times, and wished to give their children all the opportunities possible. Thus so, in spite of their supporting, and inculcation in parallel to their Francophone culture and traditions, that may have seemed audacious for the time.

Thus he remains thankful to his parents for their perspicacious foresight, giving him access geographically and accordingly so, to varied choices in his life. Jean-Jacques started writing in earnest, while living in California in the early eighties. In the process of reinventing himself numerous times, his penchant for the language of poetry seemed best suited to express emotional experiences. He then spent several years pursuing his writing in the south of France, during which time he published his first three books. He has since moved back to Canada and he is now living in the Eastern Townships of the province of Quebec, with his French wife Marianne.

He had published fifteen books of poetry to date, this being his sixteenth.

A propos de l'auteur

Jean-Jacques Fournier est né à Montréal, dans la province de Québec du Canada, fils de Horace Louis Fournier de Montréal et Gisèle Leduc de Huntington, Québec.

Francophone de naissance, il a fait ses études dans un cursus anglophone, par choix de ses parents, qui venaient de familles bilingues. Conscients du contexte socio-économique de l'époque, ils voulurent donner à leur enfants une liberté de choix de carrière. La décision de ses parents était audacieuse pour l'époque, même s'ils soutenaient et partageaient avec leurs enfants, la culture et les traditions francophones.
L'auteur reste reconnaissant envers ses parents pour leur perspicacité, lui offrant plus de choix pour sa vie.

Jean-Jacques Fournier a commencé à écrire de façon constante, au début des années 1980, lorsqu'il vivait en Californie. En se réinventant de nombreuses fois, son penchant pour le langage de la poésie semblait le mieux adapté pour exprimer des expériences émotionnelles. Il a ensuite passé plusieurs années à écrire dans le sud de la France, période au cours de laquelle il a publié ses trois premiers livres de poésie. Depuis, il est revenu au Canada et vit maintenant dans les Cantons de l'Est de la province de Québec avec son épouse française, Marianne.

Il a publié seize livres de poésie à ce jour, incluant celui-ci.

Pictures:

Photos by Marianne Dessis

Some pictures are monochrome details of art works from the following artists, mostly Pre-Raphaelites:

Sir Edward Burne-Jones : Front cover page, p12, p32, p44, p49, p74
Franck Cadogan Cowper : p87
Sir Francis Dicksee : p 114
Arthur Hughes : p 58, p 130, p152
Willian Holman Hunt : p15, p 83, p104
Walter Howell Deverell : p17
William Maw Egley : p63
Sydney Harold Metepard: p49
Sir John Everett Millais : p67, p 78, p157
William Morris : p 133
Sir Joseph Noel Paton ; p 85
Auguste Rodin : p155
Dante Gabriel Rossetti : p24, p41, p65, p 72, p 108
Simeon Salomon : p 139
William Wallis : p 141
John William Waterhouse : p34, p89, p127, p160

Acknowledgements

My profound heartfelt thanks to my dear wife and life partner Marianne.
For it is she with her creative mind, for near all my book designs,
continues to be my poetic council, reader and adviser. Thus so with
patience, that can still endure my unorthodox writing time, and schedule
abuses. Her ongoing encouragement, along with that of generous readers,
have brought this effort, my sixteenth collection of poems to
a finished book state. This again could not have happened without
Marianne, and they who so persistently support my writing.

www.ingramcontent.com/pod-product-compliance
Lightning Source LLC
LaVergne TN
LVHW011234080426
835509LV00005B/495